In The Midst of Loving

Copyright © 2014 by: Cheeraz Gormon
Cover art by: Christopher Burch
Cover designed by: Kamal Collins

All rights reserved. No part of this publication may be reproduced or transmitted in any form or by any means, electronically or mechanical, including photocopy, recording, online, mobile, any form of social or digital media, or any information storage and retrieval system, without permission in writing from the author and publisher.

Request for permission to make copies of any part of the work must be mailed to: Alchemy 7, P.O. Box 775212, St. Louis, MO, 63177

ACKNOWLEDGMENTS

Thank you, to everyone who pushed me in a loving way to get this collection out to the world. The creation of this book has been a family affair, from the cover design by my best friend and brother, Christopher Burch to the typography layout of the cover by my creative partner, Kamal Collins to the editing and revising of the books contents by fellow poet, Elizabeth Vega, St. Louis' first Poet Laureate, Michael Castro, my mentor, and fellow poet, Shirley LeFlore, and my friend, fellow poet, and one of the best college professor's I've had the pleasure of studying under, Turiya Autry to the bio photograph featured on the back of the book by my dear long-time friend and fellow poet, Raquita Henderson to my bio write-up, written by my friend and motivator, Dr. Cathryn Blue.

Much love and appreciation to my mother, LaJoyce Gormon who kept asking me, "Have you been writing any poetry?" when I was allowing the grind of corporate life to silence me as a poet. Peace to all the poets, writer's, artists, lovers of the written and spoken word, I've had the pleasure of being surrounded by throughout this journey, namely Mike "Brother Mike" Hawkins, who got me through writers block several time, Will "Da Real One" Bell, for saying to me in a loving, yet frank way in the Fall of 2008 when I popped up at his set in Miami, while I was on vacation, thinking I was going to sit back and listen to other poets, "Look, I know you're doing your corporate thing but you're a poet and the people need you, and you getting on stage tonight."

Thank you, Ingrid Bazin for those formative Miami years, and for not letting me get in your car unless I had my CD's on me; Rashida Bartley for your love, straight forwardness and laughter...and yes, the poem must make sense; Dr. Cathryn Blue for all the love, and listening to me talk it out through the tears; Montague Simmons for always being there; The Robinson and Gormon family for raising me; The Burch family of University City for loving me like a sister and daughter; To my Soul Vibe Poetry Collective family, thank you for teaching me that fear has no place in the heart of a creative. I love you all; To my Legacy Books and Café family, I'm grateful to have had a place where we all could grow, share, be serious, and love one another through our words and actions; Robert Bullivant and Claire of Bullivant Gallery, for doing what you all do with such love and care; Brother Ting, whose home was church, whose words were and are freedom, and the days of plum wine, Pho Grand, Kung Fu flick mornings with the crew, and perfectly rolled joints are the things great memories are made of. Last but surely not least, thank you to the St. Louis Regional Arts Commission for providing me with an Artists Support Grant to help make this book possible.

This book is dedicated to my mother LaJoyce Gormon, my father John Gormon, Sr., my brothers Theodis and John Gormon, Jr.

While it may not feel like it at times, the way we've loved each other has been perfect.

And, John, my dear baby brother, while you are no longer here with us in the physical, I know you are still here with us in spirit. I miss and love you like only a sister can miss and love a baby brother gone too soon. I'm strengthened by the love you gave during your 27-year Earthly visit with us.

And to Mike "Brother Mike" Hawkins

*If mornin' don't come
Every night I'll wait for you
Underneath the Moon*

*To: Ruth-Ann
Please enjoy the words.
Peace & Love*

In The Midst of Loving

Selected poems and writings by

Cheeraz Gormon

Contents

Haiku 1	10
A Street Named Portland in Brooklyn	11
Smoldering	12
A Million Tiny Pieces	13
In Loving Memory of A Young Man I Never Met	15
Untitled	17
The Night We Silenced Harlem	19
We Be	20
Our Love	22
Shoo Away Fly	24
Lust's Amnesia	26
You	27
The Great Divide	29
Beautiful Sad Girl	30
Who Moved My Memories	33
Jasmine	38
Brian's Song	42
Pieces of Me	46
Illumination	48
Mourning (Half Mast)	49
Move	50

Eyes Wide Open	53
Nappy Head	54
Her Leaving	56
This Is	57
The Sun	59
A Painful Pattern	62
The Confession	63
Morning Blue	64
(Show Me) What It Means to Breathe	66
Between Sun and Moon	68
No Martyr	69
Have Patience With Me, Brother	70
We Better Pull This Wire Now	71
Black and Blue	75
Love Like	79

Haiku 1

Her love fell rotten
To the ground from the heat while
He just walked away

A Street Named Portland in Brooklyn
(walking about in Ft. Greene, 2011)

There's a lot more color here but a lot less green. Black men actually stop and acknowledge me a Black woman walking down the street. They make eyes as I stand in line at the store. Crack boyish-like smiles as I turn around to confirm what my intuition was telling me.

For the most part, Black men rarely looked at me in Portland, Oregon let alone uttered a compliment. But here, on the corner of S. Portland and Fulton you would think I was the next best thing to air. Judging from these brothas gaze my skin was made of stars; my afro rivaled the intensity of Saturn's rings. Not too far away from this intersection, a man took my hand into his while introducing himself and I was tempted to present myself as Venus.

The air quality may not be as good here but I breathe deeper. My stride moves at a quickened pace but I don't miss much. I notice people look down to peep your shoe game, but not to avoid eye contact. I haven't ran into many hipsters in this area but I'm sure they're somewhere not too far away sharing a case of PBR amongst themselves while trading tips on how to style the most unique mustache.

From what I'm told, this neighborhood has changed. Caught up in the hurricane of gentrification with pockets unfamiliar even unto itself. I just pray that when the literal and figurative dust settles that this place in Brooklyn never starts to feel like Portland, Oregon. Never sheds that thing that makes it Ft. Greene in exchange for dressing up in the uniform of Every Hip City, USA.

On this street named Portland in Brooklyn may something familiar, genuine, sweet and rooted continue to live.

Smoldering

Save the money for my ticket to melancholy
And go buy yourself some genuine apologies
So the next woman won't waste her precious time

I will write you out of my system
Stand on stages and recite these words
To air out the smell of what you called love

Love still
Love still has meaning
Love still has meaning to me

You didn't kill that part
Just bruised it

Guess I'm more mad at myself

Mad at the salty tears that streamed down my face
Mad at the time I'll never get back
And the locks I have to change
And the sheets I have to wash that carry your scent

There will be no ritual
Me and my homegirls will not lift a glass
And take a drink in the name of the failed affair between you and I
I will not dissolve into Cabernet flavored sorrow
It's not fair to the libation to be drunk under such conditions

Our falling apart deserve no commemoration
Nor, a good-bye

A Million Tiny Pieces

There's no use in attempting to make things right
We are broken into a million tiny pieces
Scattered across the years
And there is no trail leading me back to you
More stones have been thrown than dropped
Thus, here we are shattered

Shards of memories litter where we once laid and loved
I find it hard to watch my steps
I choose not to tiptoe around our history
My ballerina grace has failed me
I'm dizzy with our kaleidoscopic reality

From friendship to love to abstruse emotion to clear denial
And we are both guilty

Now we stand here
Afraid to walk in any direction
Because with each step we take,
Pieces of us are there underneath our feet,
Fracturing into smaller unresolved narratives
Of rapture engulfed in its own flames

And this wasn't the way it was supposed to be
And these were tears I reserved for happier times
And the regret you feel
And the loss I'm experiencing
Has managed to constrict our vocal chords

And your eyes should have never been the eyes I turned away from

Now here I am with a million tiny judgments
Eating away at my heart
Forcing me to swallow a million bitter pills
Commanding me to take a million steps,
Treading upon the million pieces that were once us,
Cracking underneath my feet

and the sound reverberates through the very core of me
playing a dirge that hangs heavy on my heart
and I want this music to stop

And I don't want to remember your touch,
And I want to forget the tenor of your voice
And I wish I never watched the sun rise on your face

And I prayed for this day to never come,
this day where I look at you and feel nothing.

...and there's no attempting to make things right

We are broken into a million tiny pieces
and there is no trail leading me back to you

More stones have been thrown than dropped
and here we are, shattered

In Loving Memory of A Young Man I Never Met
for Terrence Sands

Beautiful boy,
no one told you
that this world would be so cruel,
that the cold would brush against your soul
and chafe it
exposing you to pain
your mother dreamt of protecting you from
as she watched her belly expand.

And, your father
upon seeing you were a reflection of him,
a manchild
perhaps, swallowed a deep breath
held it for as long as he could
in hopes that an empty space would make a path for you.

I am a stranger to you
but not to the ways of this world you faced
until your eyes drifted.

Beautiful boy,
You became an ancestor way too soon.
Your meeting with manhood too short.

Beautiful boy,
I hope you know that your skin was Black
but you were never soiled
as this world may have made you to believe.

Know you were beautiful, boy

You are now free
to be
what you may have always known
you were

Fly

And be

Beautiful

Untitled

If my memory serves me correctly
Love used to be pure and genuine
Now it's too many questions
Tainted with hidden prerequisites
Words fill the space of empty conversations
And we're all drunk off loneliness

Stumbling over our own feet
Landing face first into regurgitated pain and confusion
Confessing to broken mirrors that love ain't shit

As we lay amongst cold sheets
Scrolling cell phone contact lists for a warm ear
Slow dancing to sad love songs in private
Followed by an evening of masturbating to our imaginations
Smelling of our own scent sleeping amongst our own wetness
Waking to wish that the wrinkles in our sheets
Were created by two not one

Yet we confess with conviction to other broken spirits that love ain't shit
Hearts just as disgusted as our own
Convincing ourselves that we are content in this existence of secretly wanting
As we allow our egos to control us
And its bastard mistress seduces our souls into thinking we're better off afraid
Fearing the beauty of this once reachable thing
That we remember being so pure and genuine

So we follow like children that don't know no better
As we mold ourselves in sugar coated shells for protection
With bitter hearts equipped with attitudes to match
Tear-drenched pillows live to tell the story
well after the cases have been changed

And the walls hold the secrets of our pain
Because even though we feel misused by it
We still want it
Crave it like ice water on summer days
When the shade provides no refuge
We start to remember what it felt like

Love...at times cursed for all it's worth
Because the pain tells us that it was an illusion
Next time we shouldn't be so simple minded
Not keeping in mind of how it made us feel

Because trip off this, Love makes no promises—only humans do
So it ain't, Love, we need to be taking the nail to

The Night We Silenced Harlem

you asked could you hold my hand
your fingertips traced my right palm
we moved in for a cautious embrace
gazing into each others eyes

you placed your forehead against mine
and rocked from side-to-side
pulled away to look me in the eyes
you said, "I wanted to make sure you're real"

on 121 between ACP and Lennox
we quieted our insecurities
with a kiss
as you leaned me against the brown stone

the Full Moon as our witness
I was convinced heaven existed between
the space of our lips meeting

where you came from
wasn't as significant
as your presence
in my arms
at that moment

the night we silenced Harlem

We Be

we be impregnated with life everlasting
shining like stars in our mini galaxies of boroughs and blocks
where guns shot seem like an everyday occurrence
yet, we live to see a brighter day
amongst all the sadness and pain a rose breaks through concrete
jewels drop from the lips of old cats sippin' cold beers under shade trees
and we still believe like that sista. clenching her bible every Sunday
like all the Sunday's for the last 50-years
humming Sam Cooke
'cause she seen the change come
and she knows it's comin' again
with scripture in hand reflecting on the book of Job
Chapter 11, end of verse 6
"Know this: God has even forgotten some of your sins."

yet we choose to keep track
backtracking over paths crossed one too many times
'cause it's hard to let go of old habits
old memories that seem to creep with the ease of Luther's voice
but somehow we still remain happy
like slappin' hands at house parties
collecting at the door
so the lights wouldn't get cut off
and the music could keep playin'
so the long walk home could still happen
and watch love blossom under the light of street lamps

from break-ups to break-downs
all in the midst of loving
we be impregnated with life, everlasting
never forsaking what my eyes have seen

Our Love

is it all right to talk about our love?
to speak of how our eyes used to meet
how we understood each other even in silence
as our hearts exchanged beats and mouths exchanged breaths

can I talk about the moment I knew?
knew you loved me with all you were
and the first time you held me
i felt myself soak into your existence
the anticipation of our first kiss made my feet tingle
I tasted forever on your lips

and sunrise has never been the same
since I watched it illuminate your face
at that moment I found peace
you were my angel who made me realize I had wings, too
and all I wanted to do was fly with you
love you to my hearts deepest capacity

love you enough to be silent
not speak of our love as if it were forbidden
as if our truth would destroy nations/ or us

is it all right to talk about our love
this love that changed like seasons
      birthing/thriving/dying
hidden under thick blankets of secret

this love
filled with so much truth and fear
where freedom existed only when we were sure
familiar eyes weren't looking

this love made me not want to love another
hanging on the thread of
        hopefully/maybe
narrowing my vision off of possibility

this love whose secret was too heavy to carry
even when we didn't our actions did

        we pleaded the fifth

this love
        joyful/sorrow-filled, love
was my resurrection and death

this love...our love is how I never want to love, again
for we only acknowledged the sunshine in darkness

Shoo Away Fly

I miss you
more than you'll ever know
Say, I want you
more than I should want
I, feel like I need you
but you're no good for me

So...
Shoo away fly, don't bother me
Shoo away fly, let me be
Such a sweet beginning,
now it's just bitter sweet, so
shoo away fly, don't bother me

I, hear your footsteps when I sleep
I, hear your footsteps as I sleep
Pitter patter,
pitter patter on my eyelids as I sleep
I, still hear your voice softly
calling for me

It's all in my head
You're all in my head
Set me free...

Please

Shoo away fly, don't bother me
Shoo away fly, let me be
Such a sweet beginning,
now it's just bitter sweet, so
shoo away fly, don't bother me

Don't touch me that way
Don't...kiss me that way
Don't hold me that way
Don't you, look at me that way
Shoo away

Shoo away fly, don't bother me
Shoo away fly, let me be
Such a sweet beginning,
now it's just bitter sweet,
so
shoo away fly,
don't bother me

Lust's Amnesia

How soon we forget legs wrapped around waist
Sweet nothings whispered in ears
Never soaking into our souls to be remembered

You

I wondered what the next day would bring
rolling over watchin' the sun slide in-between clouds
brought me no more clarity than I had before I kissed yesterday good night

Naked limbs rubbed over the indentation left by your frame
and all I know is the memory of You
replayed in my mind like the hook to my favorite song
and I couldn't shut it off or hum another memory over it

So, my soul went on singing—
You

As I wiped the dew from my eyes
brushed the bitter taste of slumber from my mouth
splashed my reflection

You're stuck in my head

Not even the thunder of falling water pounding against the base of the shower
could distract me,
because minds aren't crafty enough to escape melody

So, my soul went on singing—
You

Filing my heart with sound, crashing through my diaphragm,
squeezing my vocal chords,
forcing its way past the small space of my lips

Refusing to be held prisoner
this sound has become fugitive
wanting to feel the freedom
that one day it may find its way back to—

You

The Great Divide

                Take half my spi/rit.
            Record in your mem/ory
                  ha/lf my mo/ans
          and never ques/tion, why
                I didn't love you
                  com/plete/ly.

Beautiful Sad Girl

No one can look at you
And know you feel like your world is falling a part
Because somehow you manage to go throughout your day
Smiling, laughing, going along with business as usual
Providing the prefect screen to the overcast storming your heart

No one seems to question that bottle of wine you buy
Everyday when you get off work
The one who says he loves you doesn't even raise a flag
When the whites of your eyes go slight Pinot Noir red
Or after your Manhattan meltdowns
Which seem to happen every other week now

Beautiful Sad Girl,
Only if you knew that you were good enough maybe you wouldn't grind your teeth when you slept. Maybe if you didn't give other people's opinions so much credit you wouldn't sit at home on beautiful days staring out the window of your 13th floor apartment overlooking the Willamette River feeling lost.

But for you, nothing is adding up
Job...check
Man...check
Bank account...check

Wanting to checkout
Because the outside doesn't reflect the same emptiness you feel within

Checking
Checking
Checking things off the list
Are you even breathing?

Beautiful Girl,
Do you know if you left there would be a void? Martyrdom doesn't have to be a daily exercise. Have you forgotten that you are loved? Loved for being who you are, because what you are is precious. Yet, I know you don't believe that right now because you no longer recognize the woman staring back at you in the mirror. Somewhere your heart got lost and you just want to be found.

Want to be found
Looking peaceful
No note attached
Because even you don't have the words to scribe this pain
This fear that paralyzes you at times

Afraid people will find out who you really are:
A fragile spirit living in a world full of unseasonable winters,
Where devils and angels look alike

And deep in your soul you know,
You know this is not what you wanted for your life

But I know it's hard to change when you think everyone is looking
Difficult to walk away
When you know some are watching
With judgment waiting on their lips

The Darkest Hour Came And Thankfully He Was There

With both his legs wrapped around the spot just above your knees,
one arm securing both yours, phone in the other hand,
your mother on the other end, as if her words translated though him
could save you from a distance.
Pressing his face against yours, tears mixed.
He whispered reasons for you to live in one ear hoping that somehow they
would be louder than you screaming,
"Please, let me go. I don't want to be here."

Beautiful girl,
The illusion is broken, not you. Your past does not make you unlovable.
The storm has been weathered though you may feel worn, you are wiser.
Place your hand over your heart, feel it beat, baby girl. You, you are
whole. Here another day to burn even brighter. Thank you. Thank you.
Thank you for choosing to stay.

Who Moved My Memories
a lament for decisions made by St. Louis City's government

Who moved my memories
Put 'em in flames
Hosed 'em down
Separated what held 'em together
Sold 'em away to someone willing to pay a premium
Buried 'em underneath my feet
Stuffed 'em somewhere that I can't see
Made 'em look like something I don't know

Who knows why folks want to erase things

I see whole neighborhoods blighted by some sort of entity

> Had it ever thought to stop
> and think about how we might feel?
>
> Or does it know we even exist?
> Or, maybe it knows and wants to act like we don't
> Wrapped us in some sort of derogatory
> Sub-human ghetto myth
>
> Maybe it's fine with our ghost
> lost around this place we once remembered
>
> Just tryin' to find home

Not attempting to haunt anything
                        But we can't find what we recall
                        What feels like yesterday
                        Those places that made us smile and have our
                        laughter, sorrow, happiness, histories...our histories
                        trapped somewhere in 'em

Where is this love I'm holding onto
Who moved it and why?
                        Perhaps, those government notes
                        that instructs us on who to trust
                        takes precedence over a culture, a history, a people,
                        an ethic...over love and its preservation

Now, should I be mad?
Because change is the natural order of things
And it was never promised to be palatable
Easy to swallow like the first kiss I remember
But can't feel no more
But it was real
Yes, it was real
Home is real
What is missing once was, and still is real

Who knows why folks want to act like we are not

Who am I now, without these places I remember?
Without my memories but in my head
And even that's foggy at times
But now there's nothing to show for what I know
Because I know what I know
But who else besides me knows it was real?

Is real
To me
And to the people who
Lived,
Loved,
Yes...loved
Laughed,
Worked,
Rested,
Watched each other's children cross the street,
borrowed a cup of sugar, knew family secrets
and could tell you when you got old enough to bear the truth,
cut your grass 'cause they felt like it.
Knew to check on you when the summers had a pinch of hell in it.

The people...

These people...

What happened to the people in this place?

Who stopped caring about the people?

But I have eyes that see...
I see the dividing lines
They aren't imaginary
> I see what stands and what goes
> What's abandoned and adorned
> What opens up and closes down
> What gets watered and what we allow to rot

I feel the old history limping its way around
I hear its old thoughts sprouting out of new mouths
Coded language, decoded in the blink of an eye and ample silence

Where did all of this come from?
This old ghost with its wrecking ball of a way
Let me ask you something ghost, what are you getting out of all this?
Why are you laying everything to waste?
Don't you know nothing new can replace what has been,
because what was, was priceless?

See, see, I got eyes that see ghost.
They see what once was beautiful, being just that—
Beautiful

Yet, I see people trying not to see
and it's all visible if they cared to look,
so take your blinders off because it is all being seen

See the city...histories torn down
Stolen from where they used to stand
Sold like they—
        we never mattered

Like we, somehow were never precious enough

With our memories buried somewhere beneath
In a city that appears not to see all histories as equal
Tell me, if we can't find something
Something that looks like our memories
Something that feels like home

How are we to move forward?

Jasmine

I can tell the damage has been done
As she runs to me and buries her head into my stomach clinching

Her 7-year old self-esteem has been crushed
due to the teasing because of her dark skin,
thin frame and resistant hair texture

I can tell that the damage has been done
because often time I have to lift her chin
to look me in the face as she speaks

And, I confess
I am worried
and I know now that, I am in a race against time

I am in a race against time before that man gets to her head
Before that man gets to her head and says, "Hey, shorty you pretty."

And those words will sound so sweet
for she has never heard them before with sincerity

And even at that moment if they are not
she will still rationalize the sound, the emotion
to make that moment golden... to be her reason

...and He will see
He will see through to her spirit
that has been trampled the majority of her days
...and she will believe him

She will believe him through all the hurt and pain
She will believe him with the blood that pumps through her veins
Blinded as everybody watches
as she defends his every actions

Because he was the first and only to tell her

And she will believe when he says, you are nothing without me.
And she will believe when he says, no one wants you but me.
And she will believe when he says, no one loves you but me.
...because, he was the first and only to tell her that she was pretty

That her dark skin was a sign of life's fullness
versus the emptiness she feel in her heart
due to the mindless emotionalist taunts of children and adults alike
(because harsh judgement is a trained behavior)

And see when he leaves
...when he leaves
She will be on the search again for that word
for the familiar actions of the first man
because when he left, he took what she knew as her identity

On an endless search to validate her self-worth.
On an endless search to validate her self-worth
and her worthiness to be loved
because no one ever showed her how to look within

Only fed the belief that you ain't until a man says it.
Feeling incomplete until he sticks his dick inside her precious womb
to validate it

Forced into a system of mis-education
False identity relation
Taught self-hatred

Running away from every mirror now because she's been convinced

And she will keep running.
And she will keep running
until her soul gets tired and asks for her to stop for one moment
to catch her breath,
to remember why she start running in the first place

Confronted by her mentality she will be hurt
...hurt to know that what she thought was self-love
was nothing but an empty attempt to get people to see how pretty she was

She will be hurt, wondering why did she abuse her spirit all over this word
Why did she give of herself countlessly, all over this word
...and she will beat herself up to no end all over this word

to the point where she can only lie in a puddle of tears
now bringing forth the issue of foolishness

Stacking issue
after issue
after issue
To the point where her castle is built
...and her heart can no longer be reached

Because in her mind, no one wants an ugly fool to spend a life with

And as she sits in that dark cold corner
just getting by,
time will pass her by

And time will pass her by
And time will pass her by with no resolve

So now, I am in a race against time
I am in a race against cause and effect
I am in a race to show her that pretty ain't nothing but a word

And she is beautiful regardless

Beautiful because she is a Goddess brought to flesh.
Beautiful for her name manifest that she is a fragrant flower
blooming in spite of.

Beautiful because she is, Jasmine

Brian's Song

I arrived in the wake of the aftermath, yet I witnessed it

To see the pain in a Black man's eyes
takes the very breath from me
leaves my soul to bleed
my heart to stand still and my vocal chords empty

Because my
Mind
Body
and
Soul
have had a breakdown in communication

I know my eyes show it,
because 90 percent of all communication is non-verbal
so I know now more than ever that my eyes are speaking loudly

I've seen this sight far too many times before
and the imagery is burned in my mental
capturing stills that replay...replay...and replay
and every time, it all feels the same

For a brief moment
the air doesn't move
and the Universe lies in confusion
because his soul is shaken
that Black man's heart is breaking
...his hope is fading
and he wants to pack up and leave, and run

And he wants to run to a place
where he can find something
that looks like, feels like

Peace

to gain a piece of mind
and his mind is cloudy
...and my body feels the raindrops that fall deep within his soul

...'cause we've feed him the belief
and the misconception that he can't show it

So, when he is angry, and hurt
        needs someone to talk
he buries it into the grave of his soul
to the point where he becomes the walking dead
of emotion, cleansing and self-emancipation

See, I have seen this sight far too many times before
and when you hurt, I hurt
when you hurt, Black man
I hurt

...'cause he has to walk y'all

He has to walk to sort out another death within his footsteps
another failure in his trail
that leave the stains embedded
in the concrete of playground, city blocks, and Play Station joysticks

That occupies the space of basketball hoops
...to be found in the bottom of liquor bottles, and blown away in weeds
and square smoke to place a screen to hide his pain

Yet, I see through it

I see through it all
...and I feel the pressure that is placed upon the concrete
for I walk along the same city blocks that you do
and I look at your beautiful Black face and I pray
and send out affirmations to the Universe
for you Black man to shed that skin

At times you may feel you are alone
but I am connected to you by God's law
and all energy is reciprocal, so never doubt for one moment
that deep in my soul
I feel you

I feel you in the ethers every time a bullet flies through the air
to penetrate your lovely Black skin, a part of me is injured

Every time a cuff is placed around your wrist a part of my body stiffens
...and baby, when you worry

My soul is uneasy
and I sit in that window or wait by that phone
to get some confirmation of your safety

Trust Black man
I hurt when you lose hope
because it's simple

I love you

Pieces of Me

He said he wanted a white girl with a black girl's ass
Street smarts wrapped in a Caucasian shell
Someone he says, he knows is going to take care of home
Where he can define his manhood
Somewhere in between her legs
And his feebleminded thoughts
And her willingness to oblige

I try my best to forgive
Pull the facts from the history books
To reason with his pathology
Strip the non-from the sense
But it's evident that he just wants pieces of me

Save the parts that remind him of the pain
The Black that pushed his Blackness into existence
Take his struggle and internalize
As if it were a cross to bear
A lot less fashionable than a Jesus piece
As he lynches my identity
With misrepresentations and slander
Soil me just as bad as he thinks my attitude is

There is no love lost for little lost Black boy
Who became a man
Stricken with a complex too complex for him
To wrap his mind around

Because his hands are some place else
Grabbing at the chance
To find
A white girl with a black girl's ass

Illumination

The world is too small for me to want you
Even if we wanted to,
there aren't enough degrees of separation for us to grow

Thus I must humble myself and settle for admiring you from a distance
Soak in the energy from each one of your smiles
Replay your laughter at random moments

Hug you like a friend, kiss you like a brother
Dream of you only in daylight hours

> *(at least that'll guarantee that someone would rescue me from the thoughts because I really do need to be distracted)*

Truth be told, at times the Universe's timing confuses me

But, now I see clearly
I hear the message, I get the lesson
Without anything being said, I know what needs to be done

So, I'll lock your smile away in a special place
your laughter will be a personal inside joke

I will honor you as a friend and hold you close like a brother
and I will cherish the wind that blew you into my life
and be thankful for how small the world has become
because if the degrees of separation hadn't been so small
would I have ever know the beauty of what we've become

Mourning (Half Mast)

Our flags fly half mast
Our children let their pants sag
We're all in mourning

Move

Thankfully I was blessed with the gift of rhythm
There's music in my walk
I've seen the way people stare
and chuckle when folks dance off beat

What count are they on anyway?
Are they listening to the words?
The rhythm?
The melody?
Themselves?

Who cares, they're free

I've done my best
to make sure my steps looked nothing like
my mother's
or my father's
or my grand's

I've tried to make a routine of my own

Life has shown me that even if you have been gifted
with the beauty of rhythm
there may be some off-beat days ahead

Just don't stop dancin' I tell myself
Even if you look stupid
awkward/uncomfortable/unchoreographed

Even if you sweat
Make it beautiful
Make people wish
They were one of the water droplets
Created by your heat

Make them wish they could smile as hard as you do
Get lost like you do
Surrender like you do

Just keep dancin'

Bow to the rhythm
Kiss the DJ with your eyes
Seduce the air
Make the dance floor/life ask you for more

Do it until you're out of breath
Do it until the lights come on
And go back off, again

Hold it down

While letting it all go

Hold it down while letting it all go

Hold
it
down
while
letting
it
all
go

And you might be surprised
That at times you move like
your mother
your father
your grand's

And all that have come before
whose blood courses through your veins

They are you
And you them
On-beat, off-beat, sweaty, funky, happy and beautiful

As for me, I keep on dancin'
because it's the only freedom I know

Eyes Wide Open
(5-years after Katrina)

my home girl's daddy was clean for 17 years
now he's back on that shit
after the storm hit
and we're worried about another celebrity's meltdown
and we're worried about Georgia gettin' bombed
and we're worried about temporary relief at the gas pump
and some how we forgot about those on the Gulf Coast
who are still attempting to put their lives back together
while havin' nightmares with their eyes wide open

Nappy Head
(A letter to him)

from my nappy head to my deep wondering brown eyes, from the petite curve of my waist inching down my thighs. see, I never disparaged the fact that my rhyme oftentimes varies with my reason. never thought of committing an action of treason against the government of my heart. perhaps, done so in the negligence of my design, third eye multiplied to seal my own fate.

if this is a dream or mendacious imagery of emotion unforeseen, shit don't wake me.

109 days of patience. 290 miles of separation. as my infatuation lies dormant until you are seen. the kiss you planted on my lips sprouted from an intense seed of curiosity. from your lips to my lips to my neck, back to your lips until our souls met in agreement.

to deny you would be like playing the dozens with a participant using sign language, and the audience only has sense of auditory capability. releasing me from my melancholy mood, lust could never be this deep. see, I got a jones in my bones that aches like arthritis, said, I got a jones in my bones that hurts like calcium deficiency. see, i never had the desire to dance with the devil under the pale moonlight, yet i marvel at the glow of you under streetlights. silhouette dipped in midnight. eyes mounted in twilight. smile like rays of sunshine, energizing me like solar energy, to fertilize the growth of my Earth. to impregnate the essence of my being. re-birthing me like Spring. Vibe...vibrating, bees buzzing, pollinating the flowers of my heart, infinitely growing.

I contemplate if you arrived to me by way of divine intervention, for i have swam through deserts and walked endless seas, yet you came to me with the ease of a jazz...jazzy melody enveloped in the darkness of night.

Like Cassandra moved me, see, baby you move me. Coltrane could not blow a sweeter tune as i hold onto the sentimental moment when I first laid eyes upon you, and this time is just like the first time, intensified with action, and this is reality. as the gentleness of your touch glides from my cheeks to my shoulders to the palms of my hands, as if the truth were written in braille embossed into my skin. because when you looked into my eyes, you realized that your beginning began now. your beginning began now, your beginning began now and you decided to live with me inside of my sacred sanctuary.

baby, now you got me, anticipating the nectar of the fruits from the seeds we have sown together. allowing me to expand the diaphragm of my soul. now I can breathe, again slow..forever.

nappy head

Her Leaving
(for Lucinda)

The Sun disappeared
behind the tears just like that
Leaving a pink sky

This Is

This is for the men and women who've made the ultimate sacrifice
The ones in uniform of jeans and tee-shirts
who've paid the price voluntarily or caught in the cross fire
of warfare that takes place in urban landscapes

For many of you the only flags that fly are rags out of back pockets
hanging halfway between the ground and the head of those still standing

For you memorialized by tattoos, tags on walls
and tears streaming down the faces of loved ones
leaving invisible, eternal canals
those who remember your loss just like it was yesterday
whose souls beg for justice and love in your absences

And there is a misunderstanding in the land
one saying you were deserving of your fate

Diminishing your loss
because only those types of things
happen to those types of people

Never mind the poverty this world created for you
Never mind the racism you were born in to
Never mind the education system that failed you
Never mind policing that stops and frisks, criminalizes, and murders you
Never mind the greed

the injustice of the prison industrial complex
wrecking entire families
as you serve decades for a non-violent drug offense
now becoming legalized
then when released, subjugating you to a life of
second class citizenry
homelessness, joblessness, breeding hopelessness
making you the perfect candidate for re-entry

Never mind the fact, you are human
That you are loved by someone, perhaps many
That you are deserving of forgiveness

So, this is for you
the ones who were never given a chance, who were misunderstood
marginalized because the part of town you came from marked you

Perhaps, if the people of this world understood
the depths of your existence
maybe, a space can and will be made
just once, someone may stop and acknowledge your humanity
take into account the unimaginable complexities
and simply love you

The Sun

The Sun has a way of exposing us to things

Beautiful growing things

Memory-jogging things

Right before our eyes type things

We often time overlook while looking down

Chins nearly nestled in our breast type days harm our vision

As we walk along this life

Many of us step in a quickened pace

Sometimes leaving us off beat

Trying to catch the beat

Trying to find our rhythm in something

A smile, maybe

Hey Stranger, can I take a moment to admire your smile?

I want to watch something blossom

Talk to me

Let me dance to the cadence of your speech

Can you laugh with me?

I promise we'll be contagious

If it's not too much to ask, can I hold your hand?

I know they say the eyes are the windows to the soul

But I want to know what you've touched

We may just find something

We may just find something

We may just find something

We've left our prints on

Right here

Right now

While we have the time

Can we close our eyes and take this moment to dream?

Hey, how crazy would it be to fall in love out here underneath the Sun?

I've heard of stranger things

But, what if?

Let's run and sweat out all our preconceived notions

It's just a thought

I can't help myself

The Sun has a way of reminding me of what's precious,

and that precious thing is you

A Painful Pattern

I have been a mountain
climbed by many
who arrive at the summit of me
ego-filled in their accomplishment
then descend without warning

The Confession

I've never had the desire to be conquered
only to be loved

Morning Blue

Let's let love be morning blue
signaling the birth of a new day
a today that grants us a chance
for forever to be lived in each breath
each embrace
each whisper
each time our eyes meet and words exchange

you caress my cheek
I memorize each crease of your palm
never taking for granted each moment shared
dreamt or fantasized
for they are just as precious
like clouds waking innocently
in pastel colored skies

Let's let love be morning blue
uncomplicated and proceeding
uplifting and grounding
firmly establishing its newness
clamming its strength peacefully
never requesting to be thanked or praised
simply to be acknowledged and accepted

smiling sleeping faces facing
unaware that something beautiful is happening
something divine is blossoming
transcending space, time, and all preconceived notions

illuminating

molding two into one
timelessly

(Show Me) What It Means to Breathe

my lips are yours for the taking
yet, I have one request
show me what it means to breathe
for i receive you like the body of Christ
that you may become a part of me
as we share the same breath
and exhale incomplete sentences
like mantras into the darkness
as I accept you into my sanctuary

bodies twisted like tantric positions
each movement giving birth to a new letter
bringing word to life assembled out of desire
and I burn from my clitoris to my pineal
craving you like warm comforters
on cold winter days
as the tease of your tongue dances upon my earlobes
gently licking across my lips
trailing down my breast

a winding road of endless wondering
to what might be your final destination

I want to be nestled into your existence
'til we become one continuous tone
spreading across the night sky
each moan birthing stars

brown skin upon brown skin
mimicking desert sands
surging heat melting us together

dripping of each others rain
the arch of my back erects
a monument
a testament to us

to be alive within the realm of ecstasy
even in my daydreams
i want to recall each thrust
with distinct accuracy

i want to feel my skin and reminisce over yours
summon the scent of our bodies joining
until my diaphragm is filled with a joyful noise

for my lips are yours for the taking
in the name of Love
I ask you to accept this offering
and show me what it means to breathe

Between Sun and Moon

Baptize me in you
Consecrate this holy space
Between Sun and Moon

No Martyr

I am no martyr
I crave soft Earth to land on
Where I can just be

Have Patience With Me, Brother
(the first one for, John)

I felt you smiling on me the other day
When my forehead and my mouth were doing that thing

You told me not to be so serious all the time
Momma, said you thought I was uptight

And while you're no longer here, I still care what you think
So, I ask you to have patience with me, brother

Keep smiling on me

Stand there silently as you once did,
When that nightmare awakened us both
to let me know everything is going to be all right

I will sit down like you told me to,
on that sticky, St. Louis, May afternoon
when I was frustrated and confused
I will sit down and do what I do best, like you told me to
as you figure things out for me

And I will be okay with that

I will be okay as long as you keep smiling on me, brother
and if occasionally, I'm afforded the ability to recall your laughter,
and that baritone voice of yours,

saying "Love you, too"-- I will be okay

We Better Pull This Wire Now

it's an ugly psychology
that leaves dour looks
on Black faces
and places salt in the wounds
of the psyche

the ancient stench
throws like an expensive candle
and settles amongst
our souls

we live with it
it meets many of us before we can get a rhythm in our strides

i've always been suspicious
of the notion of looking suspicious
because for some folks, that changes all the time

from where I stand
it's always Black or Brown
whose lifeless bodies are lying on the ground
or housed in 6x9s

Man
Woman
Child

guns get drawn with fear-filled questions being screamed
or threatening interrogation
or cowardly provocation
or in complete silence
(I have no idea if, Theodore Wafer said anything before taking, Renisha McBride's life.)

yet, all of these actions have one thing in common:
a mission to kill
to claim a life thought unworthy

we continuously get our pride stripped
camera phones capture the instances
for the world to critique
just how responsible we were for our demise

assigned guilt because we got ghetto sounding names
school records, and social media histories get pulled
placed before the court of public opinion to justify our hunting down

in this place the psychological pressure is keeping pace
with the heat that rises

and I hear this snapping sound
I hear this snapping sound
and I hear this snapping sound

I saw sparks fly from that young man's mouth
as he screamed, "WHY"

I saw his mother attempt to beat the pain out of her chest
Her heartbeat, a thunderous war cry
Her tears, spiked crystals

I saw his father attempt to straighten his back
but the pain hit him there
there, in that spot folding him in half

and I bet God is getting an earful tonight

history cycled around with enough warning
those who cared listen, we felt the crescendo coming

and attempted to brace ourselves with logic
with reason
with heart
mind
body
soul

ain't this the trippiest shit in town
Black and Brown bodies lifeless on the ground
for a relic reason

and I'm waiting on easier and brighter
easier and brighter
easier and brighter

better shine a light while we got time because our children are watching
and they got bags under their eyes

better shine a light because they doin' it all in broad daylight
and tryin' to hide

better shine a light
'cause I hear a ticking sound
I hear a ticking sound
I hear a ticking sound

we better pull this wire now

Black and Blue

This poem started in the middle of itself
Like so many of us do
Rushed into me like rhythm
You know, the kind you learn early from mother's hums
and dance routines

Momma's humming again
Accompanied by a back-and-forth rocking motion
Like she's having a concert with her emotions
Her mood is the color of night settling into itself

Black and blue
All over a lover who decided to imprint love across her face
Eyes braille, raised and hard to the touch

And I hear little girls speaking about the devil beating his wife
When the sun in shining and the rain is coming down
Like this is something to be remembered for generations

From great-grands to breast sprouting before season in this unnatural land
Where she learns early 'to use what she got, to get what she wants'
Passed down to her from women who heard the song
and used the lyrics as filler for their self esteem

Rollin' on the river
She was black and blue once too

And I got conflicting feelings about Miles for what he did to Cicely

A love supreme
Showed her how to love with a hard shell
and a razor somewhere on her person
just in case a muthafucka tried to trip

Black and blue
Rings around eyes

But this ain't Saturn

These are colors born from silence
And women who tell themselves somehow they deserved
the taps that drained their very souls

Try the new woman on tap
Drink up before there's nothing left

Women and girls dance in this man's world
Between 'anytime, any place' and 'did he just take it?'

Where does a woman go to find peace?

Is solace found haphazardly?

Like finding that seasoning you were looking for months ago
on a shelf it should've been on in the first place,
but you know where it is now
and that's good enough
but it's also old news

Black and blue

We don't have to suffer the same fate
Black
Black
Black woman
Black girl

We don't have to be the training ground
for misplaced anger masking itself as manhood

Blue girls
Criticized for rolling our eyes
Curling our lips

With words ready on our tongues,
Waiting for the hammer to drop

We don't have to be Black and Blue all the time

Can't we just be?

We want to just be.

Yes, tears look sad but are they really
I heard a woman once cured herself with her tears
Cried the sickness right on out of herself
onto some nearby pillowcase
She later dreamt on

And I'm having dreams of women and girls singing in the sunlight
Minus the glasses shading their eyes
Some humming
All dancing on solid ground
To the beat of healthy hearts

Girl, you hear that
The silence is no longer a sad hiding place
where insomnia stricken souls go to dry heave their pain
Because somebody left directions on the Sun,
'On How To Reflect Differently'

Love Like

In this day and age of fucking
I still believe I can have it
In this time of meeting the representative
Before meeting the actual person
I still believe I can grasp it

Because, I know what it felt like
And no, I'm not talking 'bout recreations of the past
Perhaps, to remember some of its nostalgia
...its simplicity
...its truth

I want to love with the patience of first kisses
and blue light basement parties
when we could only hold each other and think about, It
Allowing our minds to caresses those sweet moments

Love like, bare feet running through grass
inhaling the fresh scent of blossoming rose bushes
on a St. Louis Spring morning

Taking mid-day naps on Art Hill
waking to find you recording the features of my face into your memory
as I trip off the curves of your lips while your taking

Love like, deep tissue massages that give a case of temporary amnesia
from all the bullshit encountered during the day
Like gentle kisses across the lower back
trailing tongue down inner thighs...
stopping to play with the back of knee caps

I want to love good enough
to wake up in the morning and cook you biscuits from scratch
To let you know
that all those things
I whispered in your ears
while you were inside of me wasn't an act
or filler in-between the moans and silence
with scratches adorning our backs
like tribal markings

Baptized in each others sweat, scented lavender

Love, like that playful slap on the ass
as I walk out the door
to serve as a reminder
that I can get it when I get back
       and I will definitely take you up on that offer

See, I want to love good enough
that when we stand close
we can dance to the beat of each others hearts

Laugh like children
as we tickle belly buttons under covers
kisses leaving a sweeter taste
thank coconut and blueberry snow cones

Forehead to forehead
mouths half open
exchanging breaths as we sleep

Bathing together by candlelight after disagreements
'cause life and love ain't flawless
and times like these will happen

I want to love like
long conversations over
God
Religion
Politics
how our days went
and that movie we've seen several times before

And, no
I'm not taking about
recreating the past

Perhaps, to revisit some of its nostalgia
Its simplicity
Its truth

Simply, because it was genuine

What Are You Feeling?

(This page is blank for you to write something)

(This page is blank for you to write something)

(This page is blank for you to write something)

What's Your Love Story?

(This page is blank for you to write something)

(This page is blank for you to write something)

(This page is blank for you to write something)

What Are You Willing To Fight For?

(This page is blank for you to write something)

(This page is blank for you to write something)

(This page is blank for you to write something)

You Want A Love Like...

(This page is blank for you to write something)

(This page is blank for you to write something)

Who
Would You
Rather Be With
Right Now?

(This page is blank for you to write something)

(This page is blank for you to write something)

Thank you, for sharing in this journey.